D0178909

JOHN

NEVER THIRST AGAIN

10 Publishing
a division of **10** of those.com

John: Never Thirst Again
Copyright © 2014 David Cook

Published by 10Publishing, a division of 10ofthose.com 9D Centurion Court,
Farington, Leyland, PR25 3UQ, England

Email: info@10ofthose.com
Website: www.10ofthose.com

The right of David Cook to be identified as the Author of this Work has been asserted
by him in accordance with the Copyright, Designs and Patents Act 1988.

All rights reserved. No part of this publication may be reproduced, stored in a
retrieval system, or transmitted in any form or by any means, electronic, mechanical,
photocopying, recording or otherwise, without the prior permission of the publisher
or a licence permitting restricted copying.

In the UK such licences are issued by the Copyright Licensing Agency, 90 Tottenham
Court Road, London, W1P 9HE.

Bible quotations taken from the HOLY BIBLE, NEW INTERNATIONAL VERSION®.
Copyright © 1973, 1978, 1984 Biblica. Used by permission of Zondervan. All rights
reserved. The "NIV" and "New International Version" trademarks are registered in
the United States Patent and Trademark Office by Biblica.

British Library Cataloguing in Publication Data. A catalogue record for this book is
available from the British Library.

ISBN: 978-1-909611-30-6

Cover Design and Typeset by: Diane Bainbridge
Printed in the UK

David Cook

30 UNDATED DEVOTIONS
THROUGH THE BOOK OF JOHN

INTRODUCTION

John begins his gospel in words that remind us of Genesis: 'In the beginning'. In the Gospel of John we have a new Genesis, a new beginning, the coming into flesh of the Lord of the new creation.

In the same way that the tick has become an unmistakable trademark of Nike, so the number seven represents to the Hebrew mind the sense of wholeness and completeness of God and His work. Accordingly, Genesis 1:1 is a verse of seven words in Hebrew. Six times in Genesis 1 we are told 'it was so'; sixteen times we read 'God said' or 'called', and seven times, 'it was [very] good'. God's name is used thirty times in the creation account of Genesis 1:1 – 2:3.

John's Gospel is also the gospel of sevens. There are seven 'I am' statements of Jesus and seven signs authenticating these claims.

The major theme of John's Gospel is that Jesus is the source of the life of the new creation. We read that eternal life is '[knowing] you, the only true God, and Jesus Christ, whom you have sent' (John 17:3). God bestows new birth for the new creation (John 3:3,5); the children of God are those who are born of God (John 1:13), and new birth is the giving of this eternal life.

When we write letters or emails, it is customary to state the subject at the beginning. John states his subject, the reason for his writing, at the end of his writings. For example, in 1 John 5:13, at the end of his letter, he tells his readers he has written so they can be sure that they have eternal life. In his gospel, in John 20:31, he writes that his purpose is that readers might believe in Jesus – that He is the Christ, the Son of God – and so have eternal life through Him.

In John's Gospel, Jesus states His claims: I am the bread of life; the light of the world; the gate to the sheepfold; the good shepherd; the resurrection and the life; the way, the truth and the life; the true vine. He backs His words with signs: healing the sick and paralyzed; giving sight to the blind; raising the dead; feeding the 5,000; walking on water; turning water into wine.

John allows the witnesses to testify about Jesus: John the Baptist (1:20); Andrew (1:40); Philip (1:45); Nathanael (1:49); the woman (4:29); Moses (5:46); John himself (21:24); and God the Father (8:18).

See the signs, hear the witnesses, listen to the claims, examine the evidence and believe that Jesus is the Christ, the Son of God, and so become representatives of the new creation, living out a new quality of life – eternal life – in this crumbling old creation.

Traditionally, John's Gospel is symbolized by the eagle, soaring high, giving us the eternal perspective.

The things which are peculiar to his gospel are among the most precious possessions of the Church of Christ.[1]

---

1. J.C. Ryle, *Expository Thoughts on the Gospels: John*, vol. 1 (London: Banner of Truth, [1869] 1987), p. 1.

Words reveal and explain. So the Word is the revelation of God, God's self-explanation. John tells us about the Word:

- He was in the beginning – pre-existent and eternal;

- He was in relationship with God, yet distinct from God;

- He was God – He is eternal, pre-existent divinity;

- All things were made through Him;

- He is the source of life and light for all;

- He was generally not understood or received by the world in general, or His own people in particular;

- To those who receive Him, He gives authority to be the children of God.

We are told about John the Baptist (vv. 6–9):

- He was a man sent from God;

- He came as a witness to testify to the light;

- He was not the light, but came into the world before the light.

We are told about believers (vv. 12,13):

- They receive and believe in the Word, rather than non-recognition and non-reception;

- They are given the right to be the children of God;

- They are born of God's decision and will.

Note the Word's relationship to God, the world and the believer. Notice how John describes the believer.

REFLECTION

In 'Knowing God',[1] J.I. Packer says that in spare moments, believers need to remind themselves of their identity:

'I am a child of God, God is my Father, heaven is my home, every day is one day nearer heaven, my Saviour is my brother, every Christian is my brother [or sister] too.'

1. J.I. Packer, *Knowing God* (London: Hodder & Stoughton, 1973), p. 256.

Verse 14 is a key verse in the whole of John's introduction. We are told that the Word – the revelation and expression of God –, the one who is God – takes on flesh and becomes a man. Two words are vital here: 'flesh' and 'made his dwelling'.

In the first century, there were those who claimed that the spiritual and material could never mix, that the divine and flesh could not meet. John says the Word became real, human flesh (see 1 John 4:2).

With the Jews in mind, John uses the word 'tabernacled', which is translated 'made his dwelling'. This word recalls Exodus 33 and 34, where Moses met God in the tabernacle, or tent of meeting. There God spoke to him 'as a man speaks with a friend' (Exod. 33:11). Moses asked to see God's glory and, as a result, having seen Him, Moses himself became radiant; so much so that he needed to veil his face when he met the people of Israel. Now, John says, the Word 'tents' among us and His glory is apparent. We meet God and hear Him speak in the Word who became flesh.

Verse 15 is a bracket. Verse 16 follows on from verse 14 – because the Word is full of grace and truth, we received grace on top of grace.

Verse 17 explains. We received the grace of the law given through Moses, but that grace has been supplanted by the greater grace, that which came through Jesus Christ.

The bracket of verse 15 tells us that whereas John had earlier spoken of the abstract – light – he now speaks of a person: 'He' surpasses me because he was pre-existent.

Thus for the first time, the Word, the Creator, the glorious one is named: Jesus Christ (v. 17).

Verse 18 is the summary verse of the prologue, telling us of the human dilemma: no one has looked into the face of God but the one who is uniquely God, the one who is in the unique place – in the Father's bosom – has the unique ministry of literally exegeting, explaining, making God known.

REFLECTION

Jesus makes God known. Many people, particularly in sects and cults, would deny this fundamental truth. How important for our salvation is it that we truly see that Jesus is God made manifest in the flesh?

Again John the Baptist provides a model of witness.

A delegation from Jerusalem comes to investigate the impact of his ministry. John is insistent: he is not Elijah; he is not the prophet (like Moses). Then 'Who are you?' they ask (v. 22). John is the voice (v. 23), the forerunner spoken of in Malachi 4:5 and Isaiah 40:3. The reason he baptizes is to awaken Israel and identify the Messiah (v. 31). John is not worthy even to do the slave's job of untying the Messiah's sandals (v. 27). The coming one is the baptizer with the Holy Spirit (v. 33). John is the persistently self-effacing witness.

There follow three brief cameos of Jesus, each introduced by the phrase, 'The next day'.

1. John says Jesus is the Lamb of God, the baptizer with the Holy Spirit, the Son of God (v. 29).

2. Again, in verse 35, Jesus is the Lamb of God. The two disciples of John hear John say this, but they don't follow John; instead they follow Jesus (v. 37).

3. In verse 43, Jesus finds Philip who finds Nathanael, who confesses Jesus is the Son of God, King of Israel (v. 49). Andrew finds Simon (v. 41); Philip finds Nathanael (v. 45), but Jesus finds Philip (v. 43), who may have been overlooked by the others. See evidence of his ordinariness in 6:5 ff.; 12:20–22; 14:8. 'Jesus... Finding Philip'. Note also John's

emphasis that Jesus is to be followed (vv. 37,38,40,43).

Note in passing the titles and descriptions of Jesus here in John 1.

The envelope is fully opened in verse 51. In a clear reference to Jacob's ladder (Gen. 28:12), now it is Jesus who is the ladder linking heaven and earth.

J.C. Ryle finds twenty-one descriptions of Jesus in this chapter. He is rabbi, Son of God, King of Israel, Messiah, but now the most exalted title of all is His: Son of Man – the one with universal authority (see Dan. 7:13,14).

Verse 37 is God's pattern for saving people: they hear the witness but don't follow the witness; instead, they follow Jesus.

When Billy Graham left Sydney after his first crusade in 1959, crowds bid him farewell from Sydney airport. As they did, he spoke briefly from John 1:37 where the people heard John, but followed Jesus.

This is the pattern: we hear John, we hear Billy, but we follow Jesus.

REFLECTION

Think of the individual titles Christ is given here. Then read Daniel 7:13,14, and spend some time praising God.

Originally the text of Scripture was without chapter and verse divisions – chapters were added in the thirteenth century and verses in the sixteenth century – so the writer had to show divisions in other ways. The way John marks this section is by the bookends; the first sign in Cana (2:1–11) and the second sign in Cana (4:43–54).

This section as a whole emphasizes:

• With Jesus, the new has come: He turns water into wine; He is the new Temple where God and people meet; He makes people new and quenches eternal thirst by giving eternal life.

• Jesus knows all things: He knows what is in people (2:25); He knows what Nicodemus needs; He knows all about the woman (4:29,39); He knew that the official's son would live.

In today's reading, Jesus comes to Cana to grace a wedding with His presence. It seems to be a family occasion; Jesus' mother is invited, Jesus is invited, and generously, His new disciples are included in the invitation.

Perhaps the inviter's generosity extended too far, because they run out of wine. Mary is told, maybe because she is the senior family member present. She tells Jesus, her eldest son, who responds respectfully, 'Dear woman' (see 19:26). He indicates that He is on God's timetable. Mary's only command in Scripture follows (v. 5).

There are six jars containing about 750 litres of water for cleansing, the equivalent of 1,000 bottles of wine. They are filled and some is drawn off and then the master of ceremonies commends the bridegroom for the excellence of his wine; it is even better than the earlier provision.

Without touching or speaking, Jesus has revealed His glory (v. 11) – His deity, power, Messiahship. He does not make stones into bread to satisfy Satan, but He turns water into wine to reveal His glory. Jesus fulfils Isaiah 25:6–9. He gives a foretaste of a greater banquet. In Revelation 19:9 the same writer, John, tells us of the wedding supper of the groom, Jesus Christ, and His bride, the church.

The glimpse we have at Cana will one day give way to the eternal reality.

REFLECTION

Wine may be seen to symbolize joy. Jesus hadn't come to take their joy away; instead, He came to bring them new joy. Reflect on the fullness of life He promises. How different is it from the 'joy' people have in the world?

Today's reading begins with many believing on the basis of the signs Jesus was doing in Jerusalem (see John 20:29). Verse 24 tells us that though they believed in Him, Jesus did not believe in them. The reason is repeated in verses 24 and 25: Jesus knows what people are like, and He needed no advice about them.

Chapter 3:1 immediately introduces Nicodemus, a good example of one known by Jesus. In terms of status, Nicodemus was roughly equivalent to a high court judge, a university professor and a senator, all rolled into one. He has a reputation to protect, and so he comes at night and uses the royal 'we' (v. 2), making a diplomatically careful statement.

Jesus knows people, and He knows this man, who despite his status and moral goodness needs the birth from above, without which he will neither see nor enter the kingdom of God (vv. 3,5).

Nicodemus, like the Jews spoken of in 2:20 and the woman in 4:15, understands Jesus' words literally (v. 4): how can someone re-enter their mother's womb to be born again? This misunderstanding gives Jesus the opportunity to correct and explain.

This new birth is from the Spirit (v. 6), and Nicodemus should know of it from his Old Testament Scripture (vv. 7,10). (See Ezekiel 36:25–36).

The Spirit is sovereign in giving this birth (v. 8); the wind is outside of our control, as is the Spirit. The Spirit's sovereignty re-emphasizes what John has said in 1:12,13.

Verses 10 to 21 answer the question of verse 9, 'How can this be?' The focus now shifts from the new birth – God's part in our salvation, to belief – the immediate fruit of the new birth in our experience.

In the light of the 'everyone'/'whoever terms' – verses 15,16 and 18 – it is imperative that we believe, but in this God receives all glory, for the Lord Jesus makes clear that such belief cannot come without God the Father's enabling (see John 6:44, 65).

Jesus is uniquely qualified to teach of such a reality (vv. 11–13); He is talking about what He has seen.

Verses 14 and 15 refer to Numbers 21:7–9. Just as the people looked to the bronze snake, thereby recognizing the justice of God's punishment against them, so those who look to Jesus, the only begotten gift of God's love (v. 16), will have eternal life and not be condemned, for in Jesus they recognize just punishment of their own sin.

We are all like Nicodemus, condemned already. We are born dead and remain that way until we are born again (v. 36; see 1 John 5:11,12).

Verse 16 is probably the best loved verse in the Bible. Martin Luther called it 'the Bible in miniature'. Don't let its familiarity cause it to lose its potency and power to shock. God loves the unlovable, the world that hates and rejects Him. He so loves that He gives His one and only son. The difference between condemnation and life is to believe in Jesus (see vv. 12,15,16,18).

John Paton, pioneer missionary to Vanuatu, translated the word 'believe' by the rather awkward Ni-Vanuatuan expression, 'to collapse into your hammock' – to rely, depend, trust. Such belief is the mark of those who have been born from above.

REFLECTION

How do you feel about using the expression 'to collapse into your hammock' when trusting in Jesus to save you? Have you seen yourself as 'born dead' and now, born from above, depending and relying solely on Him?

DAY 6

We live in days of sensitivity regarding sexist attitudes and misogynistic behaviour.

One of the surprising and striking things in today's reading is Jesus' comfortable relationship with this woman in Samaria. He knows who she is and all about her background.

She is surprised that He asks her for a drink (v. 9), since He is a man and she is a woman; more than that, He is a Jewish man and she is a Samaritan woman. When His disciples return from buying food, they are also surprised. They don't speak, but verse 27 tells us what they were thinking.

Jesus doesn't hesitate to cut across the social boundaries of His day to communicate the gospel. No one is off-limits! The goodness of Nicodemus does not qualify him for the kingdom of God. This unnamed woman's badness does not disqualify her from the possibility of entering the kingdom.

Here is a woman who has had five husbands and is now living with her de facto (vv. 17,18). She has little reputation to protect and that is why she comes to the well in the heat of the day (v. 6). If she came at sunrise or sunset, other women, who would have much to whisper about, would surround her.

Twice in this chapter, Jesus is misunderstood – He is taken literally when He speaks metaphorically. Just as Nicodemus thought He was talking about another literal birth (3:4), the woman thought He was offering an endless supply of water (v. 15) and the disciples thought someone else had brought Him food (v. 33).

Birth, hunger, bread, thirst, sight and water are all used in John's Gospel metaphorically, to point to a deeper reality. Jesus' hearers understand Him naturally, on a merely physical level.

The woman knows Jacob dug the well and drew water from it (vv. 11,12) and so questions – is Jesus greater than Jacob, or is He a con? Of course, Jesus is greater than Jacob and the water He gives is not drawn with a bucket.

John makes clear in 7:37 to 39 the water Jesus gives is the Holy Spirit, whose presence in the believer is the essence of eternal life.

What a picture in a dry and arid land. Come to Jesus, who offers life: abundant, vital, eternal life in the midst of the arid old creation.

In our family home there was an old book of daily devotions that was a great source of blessing to my parents. It was entitled *Streams in the Desert*, which is a quote from a promise in Isaiah 35:6. A never-ending source of vital life is yours by faith in Jesus Christ. What Isaiah saw in prospect, Jesus fulfilled in reality. He is the ever-flowing stream in the desert of the old creation.

REFLECTION

Are there areas of your own life that feel dry? Ask God to lead you by 'streams of living water' today.

In the first century, Jews looked down on Samaritans. The Assyrians had taken the Samaritan forebears into exile. The ten tribes from the north of Israel (all except for Benjamin and Judah) thus exiled, intermarried with the Assyrians and the result was the people known as Samaritans.

Because of her past, this Samaritan woman was considered an outsider, even to her own people. Her life was hard, coming every day to the well at midday, with all its heat, to draw water.

Here we see Jesus for all people. He came to search for the lost. Notice how He initiates the conversation, 'Will you give me a drink?' (v. 7). He then offers her the gift of living water (v. 10) and, in light of her misunderstanding, explains that the water He gives is a never-ending spring (v. 14). But Jesus knows her problem and His diagnosis comes in verses 16 to 18: 'You've had five husbands and you are now living with a man who isn't your husband.' She is thirsty, but her thirst will not be quenched there.

The woman is theologically aware and seeks to sidetrack Jesus by talk of the relative merits of Mt Gerizim and Mt Zion, where Samaritans and Jews worshipped. But Jesus persistently cuts deeper: the 'who' and 'how' of worship is more important than the 'where' of worship (vv. 21–24).

Then she mentions the expected Messiah. Jesus responds: 'I who speak to you am he' (v. 26). Carson notes that this response is 'theologically loaded'.[1] The divine is present. To worship God is to meet Him in His true Temple, Christ, and receive His Spirit through the work of Jesus.

The woman becomes the messenger to her village, where she was well known. 'Come, see a man who told me everything I ever did. Could this be the Christ?' (v. 29)

The villagers believe, not just because of the woman's testimony, but having heard Jesus for themselves, they believe that He is the Saviour of the world (v. 42). This is the beginning of a rich harvest. Philip (in Acts 8) will reap a richer harvest in these parts as well.

Notice the developing conviction of this chapter:

- Verse 11: Lord, in the sense of respect, 'Sir'.
- Verse 15: 'Sir'; verse 19: 'Sir … you are a prophet.'
- Verse 25: 'When [Messiah] comes'; verse 25: 'I who speak to you am he.'
- Verse 29: 'Could this be the Christ?'
- Verse 42: '… the Saviour of the world.'

Jesus Christ is the first to bring the gospel in a cross-cultural context. Note the contrasts between John 3 and 4:

John 3	John 4
• Nicodemus: a man	• She: a woman
• Nicodemus: named	• She: unnamed
• Nicodemus: a Jew	• She: a half-Jew
• Nicodemus knows about Jesus	• Jesus is a total stranger to her
• Both have an identity to protect, but: Nicodemus comes at night	• She comes at midday
• Nicodemus approaches Jesus	• Jesus approaches her
• Jesus comes to His own, but His own reject Him	• Jesus comes to the outcasts and is welcomed to stay two days with them (v. 40).

Grace initiates, grace offers, grace persists. This is Jesus' bread and butter (v. 34).

There is a saying, 'The perfect friend is the one who knows the worst about you, but loves you just the same. There's only one who loves like that and Jesus is His name, His wonderful, wonderful name.'

REFLECTION

Whoever you are, whatever you have done, how might this extravagant grace (free, unmerited favour) of God affect your reaching out to others, including the 'Samaritans' in your life?

1. D.A. Carson, *The Gospel According to John* (Leicester: IVP, 1991).

Jesus leaves Samaria and heads north to Galilee. He is welcomed on the same basis as He was in 2:23. These people had seen His signs in Jerusalem (v. 45). He comes again to Cana and is visited by a 'royal official' – either a man of royal blood or a high official of King Herod's court (v. 46). This man has a sick son who is close to death and he begs Jesus to come down to Capernaum. Nothing so peels back our self-sufficiency as the threat of death to our children.

There are two words repeated throughout this section. The first is the word 'believe'. John places words for emphasis at the beginning or end of a clause. The word 'believe' is placed like that in verses 48 and 53.

- Jesus says, 'You won't believe without a sign' (see v. 48). However, this official believes without having seen a sign.

- Jesus tells him to go, as his son will live. The man believes and departs (v. 50; see John 20:29).

- Unlike Jairus (Mark 5:35), who was met by men with the news that his daughter was dead, this man hears from his servants that his son lives. When the man finds out that it was 1 p.m., the same time that Jesus declared his son would live, he and his household – family and servants – all believe (v. 53).

The other word repeated, and likewise placed for emphasis, is the word 'live', verse 50, 51 and 53.

Jesus gives the water of life (4:14). Now, without contact with the young man, He brings him to healthy life. The one through whom all things were made (1:3) simply speaks the word, as He did in 2:8. He spoke and it was so. The healing was not gradual, it was instant and complete: 'yesterday at the seventh hour' (v. 52). His powerful word of creation is irresistible.

The incident begins with a boy near death. He is restored to healthy life, but spiritual life comes to the official and his household. It is belief, faith and confidence in Jesus, which links them to Jesus, the life-giver.

The rich have needs as well as the poor. The young get ill to the point of death, as do the old. J.C. Ryle writes: 'Affliction is one of God's medicines ... Health is a great blessing, but sanctified disease is a greater.'[1]

The fishermen of chapter 1, the self-righteous Pharisee of chapter 3, and the fallen woman of chapter 4 are now joined by a nobleman from the royal court.

From the greatest to the least, all come as paupers:

Nothing in my hand I bring,

Simply to Thy cross I cling.[2]

REFLECTION

Think on the words, 'believe' and 'live'. Believe so that you may have life. Do we sometimes make our faith more complicated than we need to?

1. Ryle, *John*, vol. 1, p. 255.

2. Augustus Montague Toplady (1740–78), 'Rock of Ages'.

Today's reading describes the third of Jesus' signs, raising the question of disease and suffering and Jesus' thinking about it. It leads on to a long discourse in which Jesus talks about Himself and His unity with the Father (vv. 16–30).

Here is the healing of an invalid who had been disabled for thirty-eight years. The word translated 'invalid' depicts a weakness or illness, causing the man to be immobile.

Elsewhere in the Gospels we read of Jesus healing a paralytic (Mark 2:1–12). In Acts, Peter and Paul will also heal paralytics (Acts 3:6 ff.; 14:8 ff.), showing their solidarity with Jesus.

As is the case with other miracles, Jesus calls the man to activity (see Mark 3:5; Luke 17:14). From a lesser person this call that tells a man invalided for thirty-eight years to get up and carry his mat would be mockery.

The man must have been weak, his muscles non-existent. Yet, at the word of Jesus he is cured and does exactly what Jesus says (v. 9).

Here we see the compassion of Jesus towards a man in misery for so many years. Jesus' words in verse 14 indicate that the man's state was due to his sin. In this particular case it may have been.

But, as a general principle, it is much better to see that disease is an intrusion into God's created order due to human rebellion (Luke 13:1–5).

Jesus says this man's sickness is a reminder to him, from God, to turn from sin and stop rebelling. The illness is a wake-up call from God. 'How safe a life is this compared with one full of prosperity and pleasure?'[1] The Jews' response is cruel. Commercial carriage was forbidden on the Sabbath, but here is a man able to walk and carry – wonderfully able for the first time in nearly forty years – yet they ignore the sign and see only their law transgressed.

What a contrast this healed invalid is to the blind man whose healing is recorded in chapter 9. The blind man is quite clear to his neighbours, and the Pharisees, that it was Jesus who healed him, whereas this man had no idea that the one who made him well was Jesus (v. 13). Then after Jesus had spoken to him, he reported Jesus' identity to the Pharisees (v. 15). John deliberately leaves his motivation in doing so up in the air. We don't know whether he became a disciple like the blind man, or whether he was more concerned to shift blame from himself to Jesus, for breaking the Sabbath regulation.

The Jews' attitude to Jesus shifts gear – from persecution for encouraging Sabbath-breaking (v. 16) to seeking to kill Jesus for making Himself equal with God (v. 18). Their blindness and hardness is evident: 'How industriously they overlooked that which might be a ground of their faith in Christ.'[2]

REFLECTION

Are there any places in your life where you see 'the law' rather than freedom at work? Talk with the Lord about that now.

1. Ryle, *John*, vol. 1, p. 269.

2. Matthew Henry, *Matthew Henry's Commentary on the Whole Bible: Complete and Unabridged in One Volume* (Peabody, MA: Hendrickson, 1991), p. 1,943.

It is the day on which this man's healing took place, the Sabbath, which so aggravates the Jewish leaders. This opens the opportunity for Jesus to engage with them about His identity. He clearly states the following:

1. He is one with the Father. Because the Father works, even on the Sabbath, He works (v. 17). In fact, everything the Son does He does because He sees the Father doing it – such as raising the dead and giving life (v. 21). The Father has delegated the task of judgement to the Son (v. 22). In these tasks – that of giving life and judgement – Jesus is clearly laying claim to being Lord. Neither of these are human activities. They belong to God. The unity of Father and Son means that to honour the Son is to honour the Father. To withhold honour from one is to deny it to the other.

2. The Jews understood Jesus to be making Himself equal with God and sought to kill Him (v. 18).

So how do we determine whether His claims are true?

Jesus also argues as He does here in John 8:12 ff. Jewish law required a witness to testify for a person, so one person's word cancels out the other person's (Deut. 19:15). Here Jesus refers to four witnesses to back His claim. He does not appear as His own witness; there is another witness to back Him up. John the Baptist has testified to Jesus, but Jesus has weightier witness than him. Jesus refers to the works of healing (v. 36) – the signs testify that the Father has sent Him. But the Father's more direct testimony is the Scriptures 'that testify about me' (v. 39).

Yet the Jews have no regard for God or His Word. Here, an opinion, unacceptable to Jesus, means everything to them.

Jesus has called John the Baptist, the signs, the Scriptures as witnesses and now lastly (v. 45), Jesus refers to the witness of Moses: 'he wrote about me' (v. 46).

To the two men on the Emmaus Road (Luke 24:27 ff.), Jesus began with Moses, to show how Scripture testified to Him. In Deuteronomy 18:15–19 Moses foretells God raising up a 'prophet like me'. In Acts, both Peter and Stephen see this prophet to be the Lord Jesus (Acts 3:22–26; 7:37,51–53)

The consistent response of the Jews is to reject Moses (v. 47), to reject the Father's testimony (vv. 39,40), and even to reject the reality of the sign itself (v. 16). Hardened, rebellious, a stubborn refusal to come to Christ and have life (v. 40): this is the story of Israel.

It is our greatest privilege to know Christ – one with the Father, universal judge, sovereign giver of life. 'Let us lean our whole weight on this mighty Saviour. So leaning, we need never be afraid.'[1]

REFLECTION

Jesus made some very bold claims about who He was. How might you show someone who was not convinced of His deity that He is who He claimed to be, from the Scriptures?

1. J.C. Ryle, *Expository Thoughts on the Gospels: John*, vol. 2 (London: Banner of Truth, [1869] 1987), p. 282.

This section contains Jesus' fourth (vv. 1–15) and fifth (vv. 16–24) signs as well as His first 'I am' statement (vv. 35,48).

Each of these signs has come under sustained attack by liberal scholars. They say Jesus could not multiply five scones and two small fish to feed 5,000 men. Surely, they say, the crowd was inspired to share their food when they saw the boy willing to share his all.

We are not always to take the Bible literally, but we are to take it seriously.

John reports this feeding (as do the other gospel writers) as a miraculous sign, not as a compelling parable.

Similarly, in verse 19 liberal scholars adopt a possible reading that Jesus is walking by the water rather than on the water. But this doesn't explain the hardened fishermen's terror, or why John would include this account if Jesus were merely strolling on the seashore.

In verses 5 to 6, when Jesus sees the large crowd coming He tests Philip by asking where they could buy food for the people. In another example of His perfect knowledge, Jesus knows what He is going to do. He takes five scones and two fish, gives thanks, and distributes the food. All eat their fill and there are twelve baskets left over, an allusion to the twelve tribes of Israel.

In verses 14 to 15, the people recognize Jesus' solidarity with Moses in providing manna; they recognize that Jesus is the prophet like Moses who is to come (Deut. 18:15–19). Jesus withdraws, because His kingdom is not about political power, as the people thought.

The disciples sail down the lake to Capernaum and Jesus walks across the water to them. After all, He is the Creator by whom all things were made (John 1:3).

In this context, when the crowd unexpectedly find Jesus in Capernaum, He tells them that to do God's work is to believe in the one God sent (v. 29).

He makes it clear that the manna was not from Moses, but God provided it, and God is the provider of true heavenly bread. Jesus is that bread. All who come to Jesus, the bread, the stuff of life, will have nourishment forever.

In the UK there is a chain of stores called Next. In the search for satisfaction what will we buy next? The search for satisfaction and freedom is an elusive search. All who come to Jesus come because of the Father's action, and the Son assures them that none will be lost (vv. 37,39). Jesus is insistent: He is the bread of life (vv. 35,48); He is the bread that 'came down from heaven' (vv. 41,51). Jesus, when eaten and drunk, when believed in, will eternally satisfy, and all who come to Him are eternally secure.

Manna didn't give eternal life (v. 58), but the one who feeds on Jesus, the bread of life, will live forever.

Now none but Christ can satisfy,

None other name for me!

There's love, and life, and lasting joy,

Lord Jesus, found in Thee.[1]

REFLECTION

What does it really mean to feed on the bread of life? How can you share this bread of life with others?

1. Frances Bevan (1827–1909), 'None but Christ Can Satisfy'.

The setting is the Feast of Booths, or Tabernacles – a harvest thanksgiving festival, but also a time in which Israel recognized how God 'tabernacled' with His people, protecting them in their wilderness wandering (Lev. 23:33–43). During the festival, people lived for seven days in tents, reminding them of their nomadic wanderings and God's redeeming them from Egypt.

Jesus' physical brothers (Matt. 13:55), who did not yet believe in Him (v. 5), suggested He come out and move to the population centres rather than performing His signs in Galilee. This was also the cause of John the Baptist's doubts (see Matt. 11:1–3).

Jesus eventually moves to Jerusalem and begins teaching in the Temple (v. 14). In verses 14 to 24, Jesus makes it clear that He is from God (v. 16) – His teaching was God's teaching (vv. 16,17) and His chief concern is to glorify God (v. 18).

Moses has given them the law, including the commandment, 'Do not murder'. Yet they try to kill Him (v. 1). Jesus questions their judgement (v. 24). They are pursuing Him for restoring a man's wholeness on the Sabbath (5:1–16), yet they circumcise on the Sabbath, an act that was only of limited benefit to a man, compared to healing.

The crowd are confused about Jesus' identity (vv. 12,20,26,27,31,40–43), hence the confused response of the Pharisees and their officers.

The key words of Jesus, delivered on the last day of the feast, are verses 37 and 38. The Lord Jesus will go to the Father, where they cannot come (v. 34). His going is the precursor to the coming of the Holy Spirit (v. 39). Jesus thus promises thirst-quenching water – a permanent source of refreshment and life coming from within the believer. He is referring to the Holy Spirit. Notice we do not receive the Holy Spirit by believing in the Spirit, but by coming to Jesus and believing in Him.

The Spirit is given to us because of the work of Jesus (Acts 2:33) and we receive Him when we believe in Jesus (Acts 2:38). The apostle Paul deals with a deficiency of the Holy Spirit by telling the disciples of John about Jesus (Acts 19:1–4).

The Holy Spirit has been called the shy member of the Trinity; He seeks no prominence. He is the witness who points away from Himself to the Lord Jesus (John 15:26,27). The Holy Spirit's ministry is to remind us we are God's children who are to trust God as our Father and to live out the family likeness (Rom. 8:15–17). 'All who come to Christ by faith shall find in him abundant satisfaction ... the greatest of all mistakes is to try to find relief in any other way ...'[1]

REFLECTION

Think of some of the ways people try to receive fulfilment and satisfaction in this life. Christ is the only real satisfaction.

1. Ryle, *John*, vol. 2, p. 48.

Light is a great Old Testament theme. The psalmist said: 'The LORD is my light and my salvation' (Ps. 27:1). The law of the Lord is both a lamp and a light (see Ps. 119:105). God's servant is to be a light to the Gentiles by bringing God's salvation to the ends of the earth (Isa. 49:6).

John opens his gospel by telling us that the life of Jesus is the light of men, the true light to come into the world (John 1:4,5,9).

Light dispels darkness. The revelation of God is light to an ignorant and wicked world. God's revelation is most clearly seen in His Son – 'he has spoken to us by his Son' (Heb. 1:2).

The setting of today's reading is the Feast of Tabernacles (John 7:2,14), a joyous celebration at the end of the harvest. Each evening during the festival, four great lamps were lit in the Temple, illuminating the whole area. It is at this time that Jesus makes His second 'I am' statement: 'I am the light of the world' (John 8:12).

The Pharisees contradict Jesus' claim and so His witness collapses. In order to be effective, a witness must be backed up by another (Deut. 17:6; 19:15). Jesus says His validating witness is His Father who sent Him (v. 18). Jesus makes it clear that God is His Father (v. 16); He is sent by God and passes on God's word to the world (vv. 26, 28); His Father is

always with Him and He does what pleases the Father (v. 29). Jesus is the sin-free truth-teller (v. 46) and says His Father glorifies Him (v. 54).

Such are Jesus' claims. He is the light of the world because He does what pleases God; He bears God's words to the world and does God's works. He thus reveals God and so is the light.

In contrast, the Pharisees have a father too. It is not Abraham, as they claim, but the devil. The devil is both a liar and a murderer (v. 44) and Jesus says, because they are his children they do not accept the truth (vv. 37,46,47). They claim to be children of God and of Abraham (vv. 41,39), yet they are in such darkness. They are trying to kill God's faithful light-bearing messenger (v. 40).

Jesus makes it clear that there is solidarity between the Father and the Son: to honour the one is to honour the other (vv. 49,50).

To come to Jesus, the light, is to be set free (v. 36), to be a son in God's family, and a true child of Abraham, who himself saw the coming of Christ and was glad (v. 56). God's promise to Abraham was that through him all the nations of the earth would be blessed (Gen. 12:3; 18:18). Through Jesus, the light of the world, the nations are truly blessed. These are great claims and, as we shall see tomorrow, Jesus bringing light to a congenitally blind man backs them up.

What a privilege it is for us to have the revelation of God. It is the great advantage of the Jew, being 'entrusted with the very words of God' (Rom. 3:2). Os Guinness says that one of the big issues facing the world is, can the West maintain its power and presence as it cuts itself off from its Judeo-Christian roots? Guinness says, 'No great civilisation survives if it cuts its ties to whatever is the source of its greatness...'[1]

There is only one light for the world: Jesus and His Word. The alternative is to walk in darkness.

REFLECTION

Verses 32 and 36 speak of the freedom we have in Christ. If you know Jesus, rejoice in the freedom He has bought for you.

1. Os Guinness,*The Case for Civility: And Why Our Future Depends on It* (San Francisco: HarperOne, 2008), p. 78.

John links this section, and what is about to happen to the blind man, with the previous section in which Jesus claims to be the light of the world (9:5, see 8:12).

Restoring sight to the blind is uniquely God's activity. There is no miraculous healing of the blind in the Old Testament, and the apostles do not restore sight (the closest is the ending of Saul's temporary blindness in Acts 9).

As in Mark 8, where Jesus spits on blind eyes, here He makes mud with His saliva and puts it on the man's eyes. Here, the man is told to go and wash and we are simply told, 'the man went and washed, and came home seeing' (v. 7). Jesus the light of the world, thus gives integrity to His claim and brings light into this man's darkness.

There are four groups of people involved with this fellow. First, there are the disciples of Jesus (v. 2) who make a connection between the man's blindness and human sin. This automatic conviction was what drove Job's so-called comforters, and represented the orthodox thinking of the day, thus ensuring that this man had been given very little sympathy for his plight, because it was considered deserved. This is probably what made him the bold person we meet here – not running away from controversy, but forthrightly standing up for himself.

Secondly, there are the curious neighbours who are not sure this is the same man who was born blind (v. 8). He reassures them, 'I am the man' (v. 9) and repeats what Jesus had done to him.

Thirdly, there are the Pharisees (v. 13) who reject Jesus as a Sabbath-breaker who has worked by making mud on the Sabbath. They are confused, for if He is a sinner, how can He make blind eyes see (v. 16)?

The blind man's growing illumination is evident. In verse 11, he referred to Jesus as 'The man', but here in verse 17, he declares, 'He is a prophet.'

Finally, there are the man's fearful parents. It is not easy for them, for they are threatened with being cut off from the synagogue. They are asked three questions: Is this your son? Was he born blind? How can he see? They know that he is their son born blind, but he is of age, so they let him answer the third question for himself. The son's testimony is clear, 'One thing I do know. I was blind but now I see' (v. 25).

Again, the Pharisees ask how it happened. The man wants to know if their persistence indicates a desire to be Jesus' disciples. No, they say, they are disciples of Moses. The indisputable logic of verses 31 to 33 is met by personal abuse: 'And they threw him out' (v. 34).

Jesus meets the man whose pilgrimage has led him to physical sight and clarifying spiritual sight. His conviction has grown from recognizing Jesus, the man to Jesus, a prophet. Now he worships Jesus, believing Him to be the exalted Son of Man (v. 38).

Verse 39 sums up the situation: Jesus' coming causes a division between those who have spiritual sight and those who claim to be guides to the blind –whose guilt remains (v. 41) because they have acted against their knowledge and, despite physical sight, descend into ever-deepening spiritual darkness.

Progression to light or regression to darkness: which way are you headed? The true light has come (1:4,9).

REFLECTION

Are you walking in the light? To walk in the light is to have fellowship with one another and to be cleansed by the purifying blood of Jesus (1 John 1:7). How can you help others to see the true light?

The context of today's reading is the darkening blindness of the Pharisees (John 9:39). In this chapter, Jesus speaks of Himself as both the gate to the sheepfold and the good shepherd. Whereas the gospels of Matthew, Mark and Luke talk about Jesus using parables, John refers to Jesus' stories as 'figures of speech' (see John 10:6; 16:25; 16:29).

Verses 1 to 5 contain the analogy. In the first century, sheep were kept overnight in a communal pen with a watchman on guard. In this story the shepherd enters the fold by the gate; the watchman, recognizing him, opens the gate; the shepherd's sheep hear and follow him. The contrast here is to the thief, the robber, and the stranger, who does not enter via the gate, whom the sheep do not recognize and follow. Instead, they run from him.

Jesus' listeners don't understand this story, so He puts it in another way in the three paragraphs that follow.

First (vv. 7–10), Jesus identifies Himself as the gate – the only way into God's flock is through Him (see 14:6; Acts 4:12). Indeed this is the way to be saved and find pasture (v. 9). Jesus came to bring us to the life that God intended. The contrast here is to the thieves and robbers who came before Jesus only to kill, steal and destroy, but the true sheep didn't listen to them.

Secondly (vv. 11–13), Jesus is the good shepherd and qualifies as such by laying down His life for the sheep. He is the great shepherd of the sheep (Heb. 13:20). The contrast here is with the hired hand. For him, caring for the flock is just a job, and he abandons the flock in a crisis.

Thirdly (vv. 14–18), the good shepherd is in solidarity with the Father. The Son is known and loved by the Father and the sheep are privileged to be known in this way. The flock consists of all who come via Jesus, who has authority to lay down His life and to take it up again.

Jesus, then, is both the gate to God's flock and the good shepherd who, by giving His life, provides the way to shelter. That is why Jesus has come. All who turn their back on pretenders and come via Him have real life – they are known by God, and know Him (John 17:3).

The thieves, robbers, strangers and hired men are the religious leaders of Israel – those who come in religious garb, whose goal is comfort, ease and a secure pay packet, but not the security of the sheep. 'Unconverted ministers are the dry-rot of the Church.'[1]

The Christian faith is all about Jesus. The gate is not a set of dogmas or rules, but a person to be trusted and known. Jesus shepherds the sheep by laying down His life, His blood, for them.

REFLECTION

Jesus is the gate of the sheep, and the good shepherd; His sheep know His voice. Are you listening to His voice today? What is He speaking to you about?

1. Ryle, *John*, vol. 2, p. 197.

When you consider what Jesus, the good shepherd, has done and promises to do for His sheep, it begs the question, why would people prefer to be shepherdless?

In today's reading, Jesus answers the question: Why don't people believe?

It is the Feast of Dedication (Hanukkah), celebrating the cleansing of the Temple after Antiochus IV Epiphanes had defiled it in 167 BC. It was winter.

The Jews ask Jesus for more information (v. 24). 'Convince us,' they say. 'Tell us openly if you are the Christ.' Then, as now, most non-believers imply that if there were more proof, they would believe in Jesus Christ. But lack of proof is never the problem. Listen to the testimony of the witnesses. Why would anyone doubt them? Jesus says that more information is not the issue (v. 25). His works are testimony to His identity.

Read Isaiah 35:5 and then remember what we have already read in John's Gospel: a man blind from birth receives his sight (ch. 9); a man who has been paralyzed for thirty-eight years walks (ch. 5). Then look ahead to chapter 11, where we are about to read of Lazarus coming to life after being dead for four days.

No, the problem is not lack of evidence. It is that 'you are not my sheep' (v. 26). You are not My sheep because you don't believe, and you don't believe because you are not My sheep. Again we are reminded that new birth is from above. It is God's to give (John 1:13). Those who are Christ's are 'born of God'.

Well, then, you may ask, how do I know if I am one of Jesus' sheep? You will listen to Him and recognize His authoritative voice (v. 27); you will know that you are known by Him (Rom. 8:16); you will have a new lifestyle of following Him.

What are the benefits of being Christ's sheep? You have eternal life and never perish (v. 28). You are eternally secure; what God starts He will finish (v. 29).

There is no ground here for superiority. You are part of the flock because of God's mercy. None of us deserve it. There is no ground for presumption. Those who are His will listen to and follow Him. There is no ground for pessimism. No matter how powerful the forces against us seem, we could not be more secure; He is mightier still. There is no ground for fatalism. We need to carefully consider the evidence we have about Jesus, knowing that as we seek Him, it is He who is seeking us. There is no ground for scepticism. For we know that at the judgement, the one who has held me will offer His record to God as mine.

The Jews understand Jesus' claim to deity and take up stones to kill Him (vv. 31,32). In verses 34 to 39 Jesus quotes Psalm 82:6, which refers to Israel's judges, as God's agents, being gods. If that is not blasphemy (which it is not), then surely when the true Son comes, who is in the Father (v. 38), it is not right to accuse Him of blasphemy (v. 36). Jesus escaped their grasp, many came to Him and many believed (vv. 39,41,42).

J.C. Ryle says, 'The abundant evidence ... the internal evidence of the Bible ... prophecy, miracles, history ... all say with one voice, "Jesus Christ is the Son of God and believers have life through His name".'[1]

REFLECTION

Look back at the 'There is no ground' statements above. Praise God that Jesus will offer His record to God as your own. How can you show your gratitude to Christ for His wonderful gift today?

1. Ryle, *John*, vol. 2, p. 246.

This is the climactic, seventh sign of John's Gospel in which God the Father and God the Son will be glorified (v. 4), so that they may be revealed for who they are. This is one of only three resurrection miracles recorded in the Gospels (see Mark 5:41,42; Luke 7:11–17). It foreshadows the resurrection of Jesus Himself.

In verse 4, we see further evidence of Jesus' perfect knowledge – Jesus knows what will happen; 'His knowledge is infinite, infallible', says the Westminster Confession of Faith.

Here is clear evidence of Jesus' deity, but John asserts that the Word became flesh and so he places Jesus' deity in the context of His real humanity.

Jesus loved this family at Bethany, and they called for Him in their time of need (v. 3). They go out to meet Him, and first Martha then Mary speak to Him very directly (vv. 21,32). Jesus trembles with emotion when He sees the weeping (v. 33) and He is 'deeply moved' before the tomb containing the dead Lazarus (v. 38); He wept, apparently out of love for Lazarus (vv. 35,36). Jesus was no robot. He was a man with real emotions and friendships; He is moved to tears by death. But He is more than a mere man; He knows that His Father's will is that all may honour the Son as they honour the Father (5:22,23).

Jesus also wants them to believe (vv. 15,25). Indeed, Martha's belief (v. 27) precisely mirrors John's goal in writing (John 20:31).

Jesus is the true man: true man in relationship with God – who is God. Verses 25 and 26 contain Jesus' fifth 'I am' statement: 'I am the resurrection … He who believes in me will live, even though he dies'; and 'I am … the life … whoever lives and believes in me will never die.' Already in this gospel, Jesus has claimed to offer the essence of life – bread, light and water. Now, He is the source of life itself.

To support His claim, He calls the four-day dead Lazarus out from the tomb. The Jews believed the spirit left the body after three days. In other words, this is a resurrection, not resuscitation, to life. Lazarus emerges, still wrapped in his grave clothes (v. 44).

I have lived through many election campaigns and heard many exorbitant political promises, but no politician has been audacious enough to claim the ability to abolish death in the electorate! There is an element of anxiety about death in all those who are like sheep without a shepherd. Jesus has taken the sting out of death (1 Cor 15:55), it cannot ultimately harm us.

Jesus refers to death as a sleep (Mark 5:39; John 11:11); the emphasis being on its temporary nature. For those trusting in Jesus, death will be followed by an intermediate state, more present with the Lord than now (Phil. 1:21), and yet not final, for we will be without a body. When we are raised at the coming of Christ, we will finally receive our new resurrection body. His resurrection is the guarantee of yours (Acts 17:31; 1 Cor. 15:20).

Is your trust, your belief in Him? 'Do you believe this?' (v. 26)

The irony here is that Jesus' decision to return to this area, to bring Lazarus to life, is the catalyst for His own death. For it is here He is threatened (10:39) and Thomas's response is prophetic (11:16), as are the words of Caiaphas (11:51–53).

REFLECTION

'Do you believe this?' Spend some time praising God that because Jesus lives, you will also live.

This is the transitional chapter in John, which takes us from Jesus' public ministry – the signs – to Jesus' private time with His disciples before His death and resurrection.

The raising of Lazarus, the seventh sign and the associated 'I am' statement (11:25) have been given. This sign is a foretaste of the greatest sign of Jesus' own resurrection. In this bridging chapter, the raising of Lazarus is noted three times (vv. 1,9,17). It is the miracle that will create the ripple effect leading to Jesus' passion.

First (vv. 1–11), in the presence of Lazarus, Jesus is anointed for death by Mary. Judas objects to the cost of the anointing oil – being a thief, he is not concerned for the poor, but wants the money for himself (vv. 5,6).

Then (vv. 12–19), Jesus enters His city. The people wave palms – an act thought to be a sign of nationalistic fervour – and shout 'Hosanna', which means 'give salvation now'. The Lazarus sign may have been understood by many to be a clear sign of Jesus' Messiahship. Consequently, He is seen to be the one who will release Israel from the bondage of Roman rule.

Jesus' riding on a young donkey, rather than a warhorse, has the effect of dampening down expectation and fulfilling the prophecy of Zechariah 9:9 – the gentle king who will come on a foal to bring peace.

Jesus will not be swept along by popular expectation. He won't accept Peter's advice regarding His Messiahship (see Mark 8:32,33). Here the crowd is not influential; it is the Father alone whose glory He seeks (v. 28).

The ongoing effect of the Lazarus sign is driving on Jewish opposition (vv. 10,11,19). This opposition from the Jews is contrasted to the response of the non-Jews, the Greeks, who seek Jesus (vv. 20,21). Their query is the trigger for Jesus to recognize that His hour has now come. It is the hour of glory (v. 23), of falling as a seed into the ground (v. 24). It is the hour for which He has come (v. 27). The death of Jesus means glory for God's name, salvation for the lost, and the defeat of the prince of this world (vv. 31,32).

In 1 Corinthians 1:21–23, Paul describes the cross as the wisdom of God. It is a multifaceted diamond: the believer looks on the cross as the power of God; for the unbeliever the cross is a foolish thing; for Satan it is the arena of his own certain defeat (Rev. 20:10); God the Father sees it as the means of His glory whereby people are reconciled to Him; God the Son sees it as the place where He lays down His life to draw people to Himself.

Forbid it, Lord, that I should boast,

Save in the death of Christ, my God!

All the vain things that charm me most,

I sacrifice them to His blood.[1]

Jesus the King comes on a foal, not a warhorse. How does this speak to you of the nature and character of God? How might you share the grace of God with someone else today?

1. Isaac Watts (1674–1748), 'When I Survey the Wondrous Cross'.

Today we come to a new section of John's Gospel called 'the upper room discourse'. It records the words of Jesus to His disciples immediately prior to His death. The section begins with an acted parable (13:1–17) and ends with Jesus' prayer for His people (17:1–26).

We are told in the introduction to this acted parable (vv. 1–3):

- Jesus' time to leave the world has now come (see 12:23);

- He is about to show His own how much He loves them;

- He knew that Satan would use Judas to betray Him;

- He knew all things were subject to Him, that He had come from God and was going to God.

Three things follow:

1. The act of love – Jesus washes the disciples' feet (vv. 4,5);

2. This act anticipates something greater (vv. 6–11);

3. This act is an example for all believers (vv. 12–17).

In this passage, first Jesus shows us how much we are loved; secondly, how we are to relate to God; and thirdly, how we are to relate to our fellow believers.

How much are we loved? Jesus takes on the lowliest servant's role, washes the dirty feet of the disciples and dries them. That which is the lowest of low tasks, the task none of them volunteered to do for one another, Jesus does; He even washes the feet of the betrayer, Judas.

How are we to relate to God? Peter protests; he would not wash the feet of the other disciples, but would wash Jesus' feet. Jesus responds: 'You don't understand now, but you will later.' 'No,' Peter insists, 'you shall not do it.' Jesus says, 'If I don't, you have no fellowship with me.'

Peter is thinking of mere foot washing, but Jesus knows that what He is doing anticipates His death – whereby laying aside His eternal rights, taking on human flesh, He will go to the cross and give His life in death (see Phil. 2:6–11). This act of washing prefigures the greater love and the act of cleansing that is to come through the suffering and death of Jesus.

'Well,' Peter says, 'wash my whole body as well!'

'No,' replies Jesus, 'if you've had a bath and go for a walk, you don't need to take another bath, you just wash your feet.

You've all had a bath, except Judas.' He had his feet washed but was not clean.

The disciples would have the cleansing of the cross, but they would need the ongoing cleansing that would come from ongoing confession. Remember the words in John's letter (1 John 1:8 – 2:2).

How are we, as sinful people, to relate to God? By being cleansed by the work of Jesus on the cross and continuing to draw cleansing via confession, and through the atoning sacrifice of Christ.

How are we to relate to one another? We find the answer in verses 12 to 17. Our Lord has washed His disciples' feet, leaving us an example of humble service of one another.

To use Paul's words, we are to put the interests of one another ahead of our own (Phil. 2:4) and carry each other's burdens (Gal. 6:2). This Paul calls the law of Christ (1 Cor. 9:21). Jesus says you will be blessed not merely knowing this, but doing it (v. 17).

REFLECTION

The cross shows us the enormity of Christ's love for us. Come to Him now in confession and gratitude.

In today's reading, Jesus answers four questions from three disciples.

In verse 33, Jesus announces that His departure is soon and that where He is going the disciples cannot come. Peter then asks the first two questions: 'Where are you going?' And 'Why can't I come?' (vv. 36,37). Peter's questions are those that a child might ask. We can sympathize with his shock and with his expression of love: 'I will lay down my life for you.' Jesus, however, injects some reality: It is Jesus who will be laying down His life for Peter; Peter will in fact disown Jesus (v. 38).

Jesus then goes on to answer both Peter's questions. In the words of comfort that we often hear at funerals, Jesus tells Peter that he is to trust God and 'trust also in me' (14:1). In heaven, where Jesus is going to be with the Father, there is much room, even for those who fail, like Peter and like us (vv. 1–3).

Thomas then asks the third question (v. 5). Later, it is Thomas who will not believe Jesus has been raised without evidence to touch and see. Now he wants specific details of where Jesus is going. Jesus answers with the sixth 'I am' statement of John's Gospel. The place He is going is actually a person; He is the way to God by being the truth about God and the source of life that is in God (v. 6).

Jesus is the true revelation of God (John 1:18) and He is the life (1:4). Because He is truth and life, Jesus is the exclusive way to God and to heaven. Here is the basis of all evangelism. Remember, that is why John wrote – that we might have life through the Lord Jesus (20:30,31). Philip asks the fourth and final question/request (v. 8). Philip must have known that God is Spirit and cannot be seen.

Here Jesus makes the most amazing claim. He says that to see Him is to look into the face of God! Mohammed would never say that to see him was to see Allah. Jesus is the Word enfleshed (1:14) who makes the Father known (1:18). Therefore, anything I think about God that is inconsistent with the character, words and actions of Jesus, is folly. Jesus is the complete, perfectly focused action replay of God. In two verses, Jesus says three times that He is 'in the Father and the Father is in me'. His words are the Father's words (v. 10); His miracles are the Father's deeds (v. 11). On this basis, when Jesus goes to the Father, and is at His right hand, we can be sure that He intercedes for us there (1 John 2:1). Therefore, the disciples are instructed by Jesus to pray 'in my name ... so that the Son may bring glory to the Father' (vv. 13,14).

What comfort is here for the disciples as they face the loss of the Lord Jesus;

what comfort for us too. There is a place reserved in eternity for each of us. The way there is through faith in Jesus, trust in Him. He is the complete exposition of God; all He says and does has its source in God. Therefore, you can be sure He hears you as you pray in His name, that He will glorify the Father through your praying, and your life will be spiritually productive through faith in Him. He will enable you to 'do greater things' (v. 12), to see many more converts to the Messiah: 'Now in the splendor of his exaltation, the Son's purpose does not change: he enables his own to do "greater things", in order that he may bring glory to the Father.'[1]

REFLECTION

Jesus makes exclusive claims; He is the only way to God. There is no other way of salvation. Without Him, we are lost in our sins. Does this motivate you to reach out to those who do not know Him?

1. Carson, *The Gospel According to John*, p. 497.

There are five sections in John's Gospel: the introduction (1:1–18); the 'book of signs' (1:19 – 11:57); the transition chapter (ch. 12); the upper room discourse (chs. 13 – 17); and Jesus' death and resurrection appearances (chs. 18 – 21). We are now in the upper room discourse where Jesus is preparing the disciples for His departure.

Two features of Jesus' teaching here are: His emphasis on the three persons of the Godhead, and His emphasis on the preposition, 'in'. He says, 'Don't you believe that I am in the Father, and that the Father is in me?' (v. 10) Jesus promises His disciples 'another Counsellor' (v. 16) – the Spirit of truth – one who 'lives with you and will be in you' (v. 17). The Spirit is given so that believers will realize, when they have received the 'other Counsellor', 'that I am in my Father, and you are in me, and I am in you' (v. 20).

This expression of the real unity within the Godhead culminates in Jesus' prayer in 17:21–23, 'that all of them may be one, Father, just as you are in me and I am in you. May they also be in us ...' The idea of such teaching is that Jesus goes and the Spirit comes. Consequently, the believer will enjoy even greater intimacy with God than when Jesus was physically present.

When God promises a new covenant though Jeremiah (31:33,34) and Ezekiel (37:14,26,27), He promises to place His Spirit in people and work within them. Here Jesus is assuring His followers that although He will leave, the Holy Spirit will come and live within them.

The Holy Spirit is called the 'paraclete' (translated 'Counsellor' in vv. 16,26). This literally means 'the one called alongside to strengthen or help'. The Holy Spirit is God's helping presence. He is 'another' – just like Jesus, so the disciples will not be left as orphans (v. 18). God will continue to be present with them through the Holy Spirit.

In verse 27, the disciples are told not to be afraid (see also v. 1). The Holy Spirit will have a particular ministry with the apostles – guiding them in truth, reminding them of what Jesus said and revealing future things (14:26; 16:13) as He breathes out the New Testament through them (2 Tim. 3:16).

The activity of the Holy Spirit will be evident in the community that loves the Lord Jesus. Such love is evident in obedience (vv. 23,24), just as Jesus says, 'I do exactly what my Father has commanded me' (v. 31). With the Holy Spirit comes the gift of peace (v. 27) – a peace the world strives for, negotiates, discusses but, alas, can never achieve.

In Jesus' most tumultuous hour He says, 'my peace I give to you' (14:27).

Spirit of purity and grace

Our weakness, pitying, see;

O make our hearts Thy dwelling-place,

And worthier Thee.[1]

REFLECTION

Read this passage again; note particularly what Jesus says about obedience, love for Him, and peace. Is there an area in your life which perhaps you have not yet surrendered to Him?

1. Harriet Auber (1773–1862), 'Our Blest Redeemer, Ere He Breathed'.

In John's Gospel, the Lord Jesus has already claimed to be the new Temple (2:19); the new Moses (1:17,45; 5:45,46); and the new Feast Day (1:29; 5:17; 7:37,38). Now He claims to be the new Israel with His seventh, and final, 'I am' statement: 'I am the true vine'.

Israel is often called God's vine in the Old Testament (see Ps. 80; Jer. 2; Hos. 10), but she always fails to produce fruit. Now, Jesus has come as the truly fruitful vine of God – the new Israel who never fails. He is the vine, His Father is the gardener (vv. 1,2), and believers are the branches (v. 5). The branch is the fruit-bearing part of the vine and, in order to bear fruit, the branch must remain in, attached to, the vine (v. 4).

Verses 4 and 5 highlight the contrast between no fruit (no remaining) and much fruit (remaining). Verses 5 and 6 repeat the thought contained in verses 1 to 4: The branch exists to produce the fruit of the vine, and it will only produce fruit when it remains in the vine. Connection with Jesus is vital!

Verses 7 and 8 expand: As we remain in Jesus, His words (His teaching) will remain in us, guiding and directing so that we will effactually pray and bear fruit to God's glory and thereby evidence true discipleship.

In this section, Jesus has already promised to answer prayer (see 14:12–14). Keep in mind that Jesus is speaking the night before the cross. He is preparing the disciples for life beyond His ascension.

In verses 10 to 17, Jesus shifts focus and shows that just as His Father loves, so He loves them. As Jesus remains in the Father's love by obedience (see 4:34; 5:19 ff.; 6:38; 8:29), so the disciples remain in His love by obedience that shows itself in love for each other.

Already Jesus has stressed love for one another (John 13:34). Here this love for one another sums up the obedience that is required of disciples and which is the condition of remaining in Him and being His friends.

In verses 18 to 26, Jesus moves onto the arena of hatred – the world. The world will hate Jesus' disciples because it first hated Him. It also hates the Father. Jesus says the world hates the disciples because 'you do not belong to the world' (v. 19). There is solidarity between the Father, Son and the believer – the world hates believers because they are chosen out of the world. The world recognizes our solidarity with God; do we? The world's hatred is sin because it is hatred in the face of God's revelation (v. 22). Revelation turns servants into friends (v. 15) and turns hatred and rejection into sin (v. 24).

The way the Father responds to the world is by sending the believer into the world to testify in the face of irrational rejection (v. 25). The Holy Spirit, the Counsellor, is the testifier to the world, and the believer is to testify as well. Our testimony is part of the two-fold testimony – the Holy Spirit 'And you also' (v. 26).

J.C. Ryle reminds us 'true grace is never idle'.[1] Here is the fruit that we, the branches, bear in prayerful dependence on the vine – to love each other in practical obedience and to continue to testify about Jesus.

REFLECTION

Jesus doesn't call us to hate or to fight the world, but to testify to it. How will you testify about Jesus today?

1. J.C. Ryle, *Expository Thoughts on the Gospels: John*, vol. 3 (London: Banner of Truth, [1869] 1987), p. 291.

Prosperity theology is not unbelief, but misbelief. The teaching that God means all His people to be physically healthy and financially wealthy is a perversion of God's intention. God has made no such promise, and trusting in a promise God has not made will inevitably lead to disappointment.

In our reading today, Jesus is much more realistic. In chapter 14 we learned Jesus did not want His disciples to be anxious. Here in chapter 16, He does not want them to go astray or to defect (v. 1).

The disciples can expect persecution and expulsion from the synagogue (v. 2), but this is no cause for despair. As in 15:26,27, they are to take heart: the Holy Spirit will co-testify with them to a hate-filled world; the Counsellor will bring conviction to this world (v. 8).

In fact, Jesus says His ascension is to our advantage because He will send the Holy Spirit to us from heaven (see Acts 2:33) and we will be greatly advantaged by the Spirit's coming.

The ministry of the Spirit will be to convict (v. 8), which probably means to prove the world wrong, about sin, righteousness and judgement. We see evidence of this ministry on the day of Pentecost (Acts 2), where those who hear Peter's sermon and come to him are pierced through the heart. They realize they were wrong about Jesus and ask, 'Brothers, what shall we do?' (Acts 2:37).

The Spirit will prove to the world that it is wrong. First, about sin, because people have not believed in Jesus (v. 9). This unbelief is the most cataclysmic sin and the only sin that cannot be forgiven, since Jesus alone is the source of such forgiveness.

Secondly, the Spirit convicts in regard to righteousness, because Jesus is 'going to the Father' (v. 10). The Jews rejected Jesus as a pretender, but God gave His assessment of Jesus by raising Him from the dead, to His right hand. The Jews who rejected Jesus were wrong about Him and in the way they assessed righteousness. Note the contrast in the sermon at Pentecost between what God's people did to Jesus and what God did (Acts 2:22–24).

Thirdly, the Spirit convicts the world that it is wrong in relation to judgement, 'because the prince of this world now stands condemned' (v. 11). The Jews judged Jesus wrongly. It was Satan who was judged at the cross; Satan whose lies they believed. He has no hold on Jesus and could not keep Him down (John 12:31; 14:30). Death could not keep Jesus in its grip (Acts 2:24) because Jesus never earned death – He never sinned.

The days in which we live are days of open-mindedness, days in which everything is tolerated and everything is relative; we are postmoderns.

However, the Holy Spirit continues to be active in proving people how wrong they are, and pointing them to the only one who can set them in the right.

As disciples of Jesus we are to be people of witness and pray that as we witness, the comforter will convict so that people will 'Repent and be baptised ... in the name of Jesus Christ for the forgiveness of your sins' (Acts 2:38).

REFLECTION

The Spirit convicts of sin, righteousness and judgement. His is not a 'soft gospel' or a gospel of prosperity. What might be some of the biggest problems with sharing Jesus with the postmodern society?

Here the final words of Jesus' final, upper room discourse are recorded. Though Jesus is about to suffer and die, His concern is with His disciples.

Jesus makes it clear that though they will grieve and suffer for a little while, like a woman in childbirth, labour and suffering will be followed by relief (vv. 21,22).

This clearer teaching causes them to believe (v. 31), but Jesus will be abandoned and left to die alone on the cross (v. 32); however, His Father will not permanently abandon Him.

Jesus tells His disciples in verse 33 that the world is spelled: t-r-o-u-b-l-e.

Jesus doesn't allow His disciples to have comfortable, unreal expectations –that would be hateful. Wrong expectations are the problem with prosperity theology; the teaching that God intends us to be healthy and wealthy builds wrong expectations that are the source of doubt.

In 16:1,4,16, Jesus warns them realistically what awaits them. '... you will have trouble' (v. 33); this is an absolute certainty. The word 'trouble' here denotes a heavy weight. In 15:18 Jesus tells the disciples that they should not expect that things would be hard for Him and easy for them. Such trouble comes from the fact that we live in a fallen world where friction, pain and death are the norm. Trouble also comes in the form of persecution (v. 2), related to their being Christians. This trouble will be unearned, undeserved and illogical. But Jesus says, 'But take heart! I have overcome the world' (v. 33). Jesus is not trivializing our trouble, but assuring us that our troubles will not overcome us, for He has overcome them.

Here, as elsewhere, John shows us that there are two ways of looking at things.

The world:

Is a brute, a source of stress and persecution (16:33);

Is loved of God (3:16).

The cross:

Place of barbarism and cruelty, place of death of history's most innocent;

Place where the conquered becomes the conqueror and overcomes the world (1 John 4:4; 5:4).

Trouble:

Major catastrophe, tragedy or irritant;

The means God uses to make and mould character (Luke 13:3,5; Heb. 12:7–11).

Life:

Trouble, stress, persecution;

Peace, sustained.

People:

Sheep without a shepherd;

Shepherd cared for, sustained and strengthened

All people:

In the world; alone;

In the world; in Christ.

Be still, my soul, thy best, thy heavenly friend

Through thorny ways leads to a joyful end.[1]

REFLECTION

Do you think our evangelism may lead some to believe that 'Jesus will give you a good life' rather than what He actually promised? What can you do to make your own personal (and church) outreach more authentic?

1. Katharina Von Schlegel (1697–1768), 'Be Still, My Soul'.

 **DAY 25**

The upper room discourse that began with an acted parable (13:1–17) now ends with our intercessor interceding.

Here is Jesus praying for others as He approaches His time of suffering.

He addresses His prayer to His Father (v. 1). This is consistent with every one of His recorded prayers.

Jesus is 'other-centric'. His concern is to glorify His Father (v. 1) and to win eternal life for those God has given Him (v. 2). He is the true servant. He prays for Himself, His vindication – that His pre-existent glory would be restored. Such vindication would glorify the Father and the Son.

These themes, praying to the Father, the honouring of His name, the doing of His will, are all themes of the Lord's prayer in this chapter.

Jesus rehearses what He has done and prays for His disciples. He prays for:

- Protection (vv. 11,15);

- Unity – just as the Son and the Father are one, so also their organic unity will be the disciples' (v. 11);

- Full measure of joy (v. 13);

- Separated by the truth of the Word from the attraction of the world (v. 17).

For all believers through the ages He prays similarly (v. 23): for their complete unity together and for the complete unity of the Father, the Son and the disciple, so that the world may know that Jesus has been sent by the Father to love them as the Father loves Him.

This unity is not to be at the expense of truth, as it often is these days. This unity takes its pattern from the unity of the Father and the Son. Notice it is an evangelical unity (v. 21). This visible unity, by the Spirit, of the disciples of Jesus is to elicit a positive response to the church in its mission. Unity in the local church, of people of such diversity, is an effective witness as to the power of the gospel. We have different colours, cultures, education, wealth levels, politics and hobbies and yet, we are one in Christ (Gal. 3:26–29; Eph. 4:3).

But such unity must surely have a wider relevance beyond our local church and denomination, so that we look for occasions to express our unity with our brothers and sisters, faithful followers of Christ gathering elsewhere.

Just as our prayers are eternally effective, this prayer of Jesus, the righteous mediator, continues to sound in the hearing of God.

REFLECTION

It is said that our prayers are our creeds. Do you pray? What do you pray?

This is the record of the arrest (18:1–11), trial (18:12–14,19–24,28–40) and sentencing (19:1–16) of the Lord Jesus. Here is an eyewitness account (19:35).

Judas carries out his act of betrayal (see 13:27–30) and here Jesus is arrested by the soldiers and officials. But even as dark as this seems, Jesus knows that God is working out His purpose. John 18:4 closely parallels 13:1 and 3 and yet Peter – just as he had in Mark 8:32 so now – in his impetuousness resists the purpose of God.

Jesus invites His arrest and ensures the protection of His own, to fulfil His own words spoken in John 6:39.

The legal process begins with Jesus being taken in to Annas (vv. 12–14,19–23) the previous high priest, deposed by the Romans. Next, Jesus is taken to Annas's son-in-law, the current high priest, Caiaphas (v. 24). Then Jesus is sent from the Jewish authorities to the Roman authority, Pontius Pilate. Here the clear double standard of the Jews is evident: they could not become ceremonially unclean by entering the governor's residence on the Sabbath, but they wanted Jesus executed on the basis of their accusation (vv. 28–30).

Pilate examines Jesus and Jesus responds that His kingship and kingdom are not of this world (v. 36).

Pilate declares the innocence of Jesus (v. 38). When Jesus dies, therefore, His will be an undeserved death. The Jewish guilt is compounded in that they choose the release of a guilty rebel, Barabbas, in the place of Jesus (v. 40).

The Lord Jesus is flogged and mocked. Pilate, for the second and third time, declares Him innocent (19:4,6). There is no criminal record hanging over the Lord Jesus. This three-fold declaration of innocence is paralleled by Paul's experience before the Roman tribunal where, three times, in the face of Jewish accusation, he is declared innocent (Acts 23:29; 25:25; 26:32).

The persistence of the Jews wins out over the weak-willed Pilate who, though declaring Jesus innocent and referring to Him three times as King (18:39; 19:14,15), abandons Jesus and allows Him to be treated as though He were guilty.

Jesus is clear in His trust in His Father. Pilate does not control His destiny, rather His Father does (v. 11), but this does not relieve the guilt of His betrayer.

This is exactly how the early church understood the death of Jesus. In His sermon at Pentecost, Peter declares that what happened to Jesus was in 'God's set purpose and foreknowledge' (Acts 2:23). The church saw the activity of Herod and Pilate as fulfilling the rage of the nations against God's anointed (Acts 4:25–27).

Here is further evidence of the sovereign rule of God. Joseph could say to his brothers, 'You intended to harm me, but God intended it for good ...' (Gen. 50:20). From the crucifixion of His Son – the unjust, the cruel – God was bringing the greatest good.

The anointed today – believers, you and me – know similarly that God is at work in all things for our good, the good of those who love Him and have been called by Him. The good He works to achieve is that we should be conformed to the image of His Son (Rom. 8:28,29).

God is sovereign. God rules. God can bring great good from the evil intentions of humankind. The cross is proof of that.

Here in the darkest hour is the greatest comfort to us.

REFLECTION

Are you travelling a hard road at present? Remember the cross is proof that God can bring great good from difficult times.

When hearing that Jesus was to leave them, Peter promised to lay down his life for Him. However, Jesus tells Peter that before dawn, Peter will deny Him three times (John 13:37,38).

Things are at their darkest hour in John 18. Jesus is betrayed, arrested, mocked, whipped, deserted and crucified.

Jesus is cross-examined by Annas and Pontius Pilate. Peter, however, is cross-examined by a girl at the door to the high priest's courtyard (v. 17); questioned by another in the courtyard (v. 25), and then challenged by one of the high priest's servants (v. 26).

- The girl: 'You are not one of his disciples, are you?' (v. 17,25).

- The person in the courtyard: 'Didn't I see you with him in the olive grove?' (v, 26).

- Peter's response twice: 'I am not' (vv. 17,25).

- And finally: 'Again Peter denied it'.

- '... and at that moment a cock began to crow' (v. 27).

Jesus' most vocal supporter denies any knowledge of Him, three times.

Jesus knew this was to happen and from Peter, one of the intimate three – Peter, James and John.

No doubt the other disciple with Peter was also known as a disciple of Jesus.

Peter may well have lied, either to gain entry or because he knew he was guilty of being the one who cut off the ear of the high priest's servant (18:10).

D.A. Carson observes, 'once performed [the denial], it was easy to repeat, with rising vehemence.'[1]

What a reassuring episode this is for us, that despite our vows to the contrary, we often fall short of our own commitments. Ecclesiastes' word is wise: 'Do not be quick with your mouth, do not be hasty in your heart to utter anything before God. God is in heaven and you are on earth, so let your words be few' (Eccl. 5:2). Be careful of the self-sufficiency that lies at the heart of such vows, because such self-sufficiency is insufficiency.

The grace of the Lord Jesus, in His three-fold reinstatement of Peter the denier (John 21:15 ff.), means that all of us, no matter what form our failure takes, will find the rich grace of restoration in the Lord Jesus, the good shepherd.

'So as Jesus testifies faithfully Peter denies pathetically.'[2] 'John has constructed a dramatic contrast wherein Jesus stands up to his questioners and denies nothing, while Peter comes before his questioners and denies everything.'[3]

Thine I am, O Lord, for ever
To Thy service set apart;
Suffer me to leave Thee never;
Seal Thine image on my heart.[4]

1. Carson, *The Gospel According to John*, p. 583.
2. B. Milne, *The Message of John: Here is Your King* (Leicester: IVP, 1993), p. 259.
3. R.E. Brown, *The Gospel According to John, XIII-XXI: Introduction, Translation and Notes* (London: Geoffrey Chapman, 1966), p. 842.
4. John Burton (1803–77), 'Savior, While My Heart is Tender'.

REFLECTION

Do you feel you've failed the Lord? Bring it to Him, so He can reinstate you. Is there any self-sufficiency in your life that you need to surrender to the one who is all-sufficient?

The prerequisite of a real resurrection from the dead is a real death, not just a health setback. John goes to great lengths to assert the real death of Jesus. He tells us three times that Jesus was in the charge of professional executioners – the soldiers:

- Pilate handed Jesus over and the soldiers took charge of Him (v. 16);

- The soldiers cast lots for His clothing – 'this is what the soldiers did' (v. 24);

- The soldiers recognized Jesus was dead and, instead of breaking His legs, speared His side (v. 34).

Yet John also shows us that Jesus wasn't really under the control of the executioners. The soldiers were unconsciously acting according to a higher purpose – God's predetermined plan (Acts 2:23; 4:28). John tells us that the treatment of Jesus' clothing (v. 24), His last words (v. 28) and His spearing (vv. 36,37) were all in fulfilment of Scripture.

It is clear that Jesus was certainly dead. The soldiers knew it (v. 33), the sudden flow of blood and water indicated it (v. 34), and Joseph and Nicodemus acted upon it by preparing Jesus' body for burial and burying Him (vv. 40–42). John also adds his eyewitness testimony as verification (v. 35).

There will always be the Bible critics and others who claim that this material is fantasy, myth, or legend. C.S. Lewis, who was a professor of poetry at Oxford University and knew a great deal about fables – the Chronicles of Narnia which he authored are a good example of fable – said that if a critic told him something in a Gospel was romance or a legend, he would want to know how many romances and legends the man had read; Lewis had been reading poems, legends, myths and romances all his life and knew what they were like. He knew that not one of them was like what was in the Gospels.[1]

John's Gospel is not easily written off. It reads as history and many early manuscripts attest it. There are more early manuscripts of John's Gospel that are closer to the original than early evidence attesting any other ancient writing. The apostle Paul summed up the Christian gospel when he wrote to the Corinthians that:

Christ died,

He was so dead He was buried,

He was raised, and

He appeared.

(see 1 Cor. 15:4–8)

One of Jesus' appearances was to His half-brother James, who had earlier believed Jesus was insane (Mark 3:21), but now describes himself as a 'servant of God and of the Lord Jesus Christ' (Jas. 1:1).

What would your brother have to do, to prove to you that He was God? James's brother really rose from a real death.

REFLECTION

Jesus was really dead. And now He really is alive. Think about the impact this must have had on James, who had not believed His brother to be the Son of God. What impact does this truth have on you?

1. C.S. Lewis, *Fern-seed and Elephants and Other Essays on Christianity* (London: Fount, reprint edn 1975).

H ere are the facts:

An empty tomb (vv. 1–9);

An appearance to Mary Magdalene (vv. 10–18);

An appearance to the disciples (vv. 19–23);

A second appearance to the disciples, especially Thomas (vv. 24–29); and

A third appearance to the disciples and a catch of 153 fish (21:4–14).

Why wasn't Thomas with the others when Jesus first appeared to them? Perhaps he was like some people who would rather be alone to ponder events than with others, to talk them through.

When the others told Thomas they had seen the Lord, he was sceptical. He knew all about wishful thinking and optical illusions. He wanted the proof that only touch and sight could give (v. 25), otherwise he would remain unbelieving.

Jesus appears again and, knowing of Thomas's statement, deals sympathetically with the doubter by offering His hands and side and urging Him to 'Stop doubting and believe' (v. 27). Thomas does that and then he declares that Jesus is 'My Lord and my God!' He believes (v. 28).

By good tradition, Thomas took the gospel to India, where he was martyred. The doubter came to firm belief via the resurrection of Christ.

True belief has two characteristics: a conviction about who Jesus is and a commitment to Him in everyday living.

John says he could have written of many more signs (v. 30) but has provided evidence, through the written record of the signs in his gospel, as the basis of belief in Jesus and thus the reality of having life in His name. Christianity is evidence based, leading to faith in Jesus (conviction and commitment) and the result is life in relationship with God that is endless (a new quality and quantity of life). John is writing evangelistically, but probably also to encourage believers to keep believing.

Of all the miraculous signs in the gospel, the last is the most compelling –Jesus dies and is raised, making no concession to death. Calvin called the resurrection the most important article of our faith. He wrote of it, 'The glory of his resurrection … caused his death itself to be a splendid triumph.'[1]

John's Gospel, which begins by affirming the deity of Jesus (1:1,14), now draws to a close with this affirmation, Lord and God, and the repeated pronoun, *my* Lord and *my* God.

REFLECTION

Are you convicted of who Jesus is? Have you made a commitment to Him in your everyday life?

   1. J. Calvin, *Commentary on the Gospel according to John* vol, 2, p. 213.

This final chapter of John's Gospel reminds us of the effective pastoral work of the Lord Jesus.

Mention has already been made of His approachability, sensitivity and His perfect knowledge and insight into the character of people. He is, after all, the one through whom all things were made (1:3) and 'he knew what was in man' (2:25).

In this chapter Jesus appears for the third time to His disciples, but this time it was in their world – the world of the fisherman.

They had caught nothing (v. 3). He redirects their netting and the result is a huge catch. John reports with eyewitness vividness it was 153 fish (v. 11). Elsewhere the net breaks (Luke 5:1–11). Here it is full, but intact.

Jesus has promised to make the disciples 'fishers of men' (Mark 1:17). What an encouragement to know that He will direct their mission, and its fruitfulness will depend on the risen and soon to be ascended Saviour, who is Himself the director of the church's life – God being the great evangelist, the great missionary.

Jesus, the sensitive pastor, now restores the thrice-denying Peter with the three-fold repetition, 'Do you love me?' (See vv. 15,16,17).

The NIV (1984) renders the first two questions 'truly love' and the third 'love', to reflect the two different verbs Jesus uses. The last time Peter was at a fire (John 18:25) he denied Jesus; now he affirms his love for Christ. Peter's sin must be faced and dealt with, even if the dealing with it is hurtful (v. 17). Failure is never final with God. Here is the condition of fruitful service; dealing with sin.

For Peter the outflow of such love for Christ is seen in his care for the sheep. Jesus is the good shepherd (10:11,14), Peter calls Him the 'Chief Shepherd' (1 Pet. 5:4) but sees his own role with his fellow elders as being shepherds of God's flock (1 Pet. 5:1,2). Likewise, Paul exhorts the elders at Ephesus to be shepherds of the church of God and to first keep watch over themselves and then the sheep (Acts 20:28).

Paul makes it clear that such shepherding is Word-based – preaching and teaching (Acts 20:20), declaring (Acts 20:21), testifying (Acts 20:24) and proclaiming (Acts 20:27).

Peter's life would now be a life of shepherding God's flock, culminating in his own martyrdom (v. 18); tradition has it as AD 64 in Rome and that he counted himself unworthy to be crucified as his master, so his cross was inverted and he was crucified head down.

John concludes his gospel by correcting a rumour that he may be alive at the coming again of Christ (v. 23). John's ministry will be different to Peter's. He will outlive Peter by nearly thirty years and die, probably of old age, in exile on the isle of Patmos. '… what is that to you?' Jesus directs the mission; He is Lord of the church; He directs each into their particular field of productivity. We can trust Him with our lives of service.

John asserts the trustworthiness of his record while recognizing that it is not exhaustive (vv. 24,25). This is similar to the statements in 19:35 and John's first letter 1:1–4.

Gregory the Great said of the book of Job that in it 'a lamb can paddle and an elephant can swim' – this applies equally to John's Gospel.

I trust you have not found yourself out of your depth, but have reasserted your faith in Jesus, the Christ, the Son of God, and so believing have life in relationship with God the Father; a life that will never end.

The king of love my shepherd is,

Whose goodness faileth never;

I nothing lack if I am his

And he is mine for ever.[1]

REFLECTION

Think of the 'I am' statements; write them down and meditate on them for a while. Has your faith been deepened through this study? How might that affect your relationship with God and others, your work, your ministry – your life?

1. H.W. Baker (1821–77), 'The King of Love my Shepherd Is'.

MORE IN THIS SERIES

ROMANS: Momentous News
By David Cook
ISBN: 978-1-906173-24-1

MARK: The Suffering Servant
By Jeremy McQuoid
ISBN: 978-1-906173-55-5

ACTS: To the Ends of the Earth
By David Cook
ISBN: 978-1-909611-02-3

1 THESSALONIANS: Living for Jesus
By Julia Marsden
ISBN: 978-1-906173-67-8

DANIEL: Far From Home
By Justin Mote
ISBN: 978-1-906173-68-5

To place an order call: **0844 879 3243** email: **sales@10ofthose.com**
or order online: **www.10ofthose.com**

10Publishing is the publishing house of **10ofThose**. It is committed to producing quality Christian resources that are biblical and accessible.

www.10ofthose.com is our online retail arm selling thousands of quality books at discounted prices. We also service many church bookstalls and can help your church to set up a bookstall. Single and bulk purchases welcome.

For information contact: **sales@10ofthose.com** or check out our website: **www.10ofthose.com**